All Together

PROGRAM AUTHORS

James A. Banks
Kevin P. Colleary
Linda Greenow
Walter C. Parker
Emily M. Schell
Dinah Zike

CONTRIBUTORS

Raymond C. Jones
Irma M. Olmedo

 Macmillan/McGraw-Hill

Economics

PROGRAM AUTHORS

James A. Banks, Ph.D.
Kerry and Linda Killinger Professor
  of Diversity Studies and Director, Center
  for Multicultural Education
University of Washington
Seattle, Washington

Kevin P. Colleary, Ed.D.
Curriculum and Teaching Department
Graduate School of Education
Fordham University
New York, New York

Linda Greenow, Ph.D.
Associate Professor and Chair
Department of Geography
State University of New York at New Paltz
New Paltz, New York

Walter C. Parker, Ph.D.
Professor of Social Studies Education,
  Adjunct Professor of Political Science
University of Washington
Seattle, Washington

Emily M. Schell, Ed.D.
Visiting Professor, Teacher Education
San Diego State University
San Diego, California

Dinah Zike
Educational Consultant
Dinah-Mite Activities, Inc.
San Antonio, Texas

CONTRIBUTORS

Raymond C. Jones, Ph.D.
Director of Secondary Social Studies
  Education
Wake Forest University
Winston-Salem, North Carolina

Irma M. Olmedo
Associate Professor
University of Illinois-Chicago
College of Education
Chicago, Illinois

HISTORIANS/SCHOLARS

Larry Dale, Ph.D.
Director, Center for Economic Education
Arkansas State University
Jonesboro, Arkansas

GRADE LEVEL REVIEWERS

Robin Bastolla
First Grade Teacher
Warnsdorfer School
East Brunswick, New Jersey

Kathleen Rose
First Grade Teacher
Bellerive Elementary School
St. Louis, Missouri

Amy Zewicki
First Grade Teacher
Jefferson Elementary School
Appleton, Wisconsin

EDITORIAL ADVISORY BOARD

Bradley R. Bakle
Assistant Superintendent
East Allen County Schools
New Haven, Indiana

Marilyn Barr
Assistant Superintendent for Instruction
Clyde-Savannah Central School
Clyde, New York

Lisa Bogle
Elementary Coordinator, K-5
Rutherford County Schools
Murfreesboro, Tennessee

Janice Buselt
Campus Support, Primary and ESOL
Wichita Public Schools
Wichita, Kansas

Kathy Cassioppi
Social Studies Coordinator
Rockford Public Schools, District 205
Rockford, Illinois

Denise Johnson, Ph.D.
Social Studies Supervisor
Knox County Schools
Knoxville, Tennessee

Steven Klein, Ph.D.
Social Studies Coordinator
Illinois School District U-46
Elgin, Illinois

Sondra Markman
Curriculum Director
Warren Township Board of Education
Warren Township, New Jersey

Cathy Nelson
Social Studies Coordinator
Columbus Public Schools
Columbus, Ohio

Holly Pies
Social Studies Coordinator
Vigo County Schools
Terre Haute, Indiana

Avon Ruffin
Social Studies County Supervisor
Winston-Salem/Forsyth Schools
Lewisville, North Carolina

Chuck Schierloh
Social Studies Curriculum Team Leader
Lima City Schools
Lima, Ohio

Bob Shamy
Social Studies Supervisor
East Brunswick Public Schools
East Brunswick, New Jersey

Judy Trujillo
Social Studies Coordinator
Columbia Missouri School District
Columbia, Missouri

Gayle Voyles
Director of the Center for Economic
  Education
Kansas City School District
Kansas City, Missouri

Todd Wigginton
Coordinator of Social Studies K-12
Metropolitan Nashville Public Schools
Nashville, Tennessee

Students with print disabilities may be eligible to obtain an accessible, audio version of the pupil edition of this textbook. Please call Recording for the Blind & Dyslexic at 1-800-221-4792 for complete information.

The McGraw-Hill Companies

Copyright © 2009 by The McGraw-Hill Companies, Inc. All rights reserved. Except as permitted under the United States Copyright Act, no part of this publication may be reproduced or distributed in any form or by any means, or stored in a database or retrieval system, without prior permission of the publisher.
Send all inquires to: Macmillan/McGraw-Hill, 8787 Orion Place, Columbus, OH 43240-4027

MHID 0-02-152398-3   ISBN 978-0-02-152398-6   Printed in the United States of America

2 3 4 5 6 7 8 9 10   058/043   13 12 11 10 09 08

All Together

Table of Contents

Unit 4 All About Work

Skills and Features

Maps

All About Work

People, Places, and Events

School Workers

School workers help children learn in school.

For more about People, Places, and Events, visit
www.macmillanmh.com

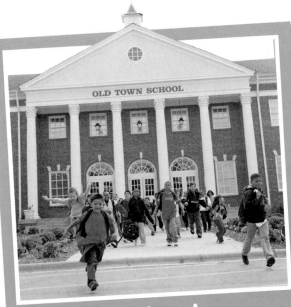

School

School workers work in a **school**.

Serving Lunch

These school workers **serve lunch** to the children.

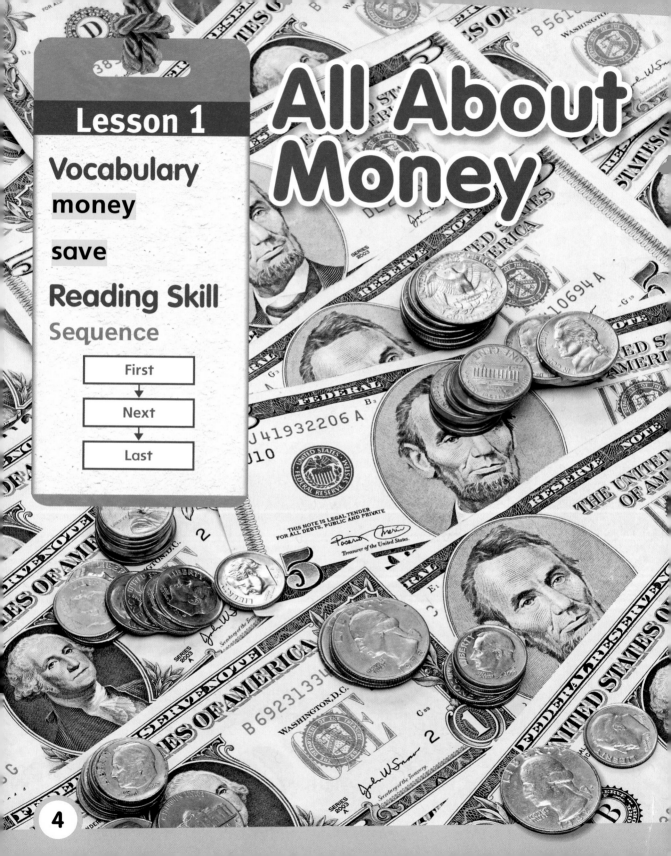

Lesson 1

Vocabulary

money

save

Reading Skill

Sequence

First
↓
Next
↓
Last

All About Money

What Is Money?

Money is something you use to buy things. Money can be paper bills or coins. Look at the paper bills. Can you name them?

Look at the coins. Do you see a quarter, a dime, a nickel and a penny?

 What are some kinds of money?

Places
United States Mint

A mint is a place where coins are made. This mint is located in Philadelphia, Pennsylvania.

Saving Money

Sometimes we don't have enough money. There is something we can do about it! We can **save** money. To save means to put something away to use later. David wants to buy a bike. He saves his money in a piggy bank.

Every month David takes his money to a big bank on Main Street. Soon, David will be able to buy a new bike.

 What does save mean?

Check Understanding

1. **Vocabulary** What is **money**?

2. **Sequence** How does David save money?

First
Next
Last

3. How does money help people?

Citizenship

Democracy in Action

Being Honest

Being honest means to care about the truth. If you are honest, you can be a good friend. Read what happened when Jane told Jamal she found a dollar.

Look! I found a dollar!

Jamal helped Jane to be honest.
What would you do?

Emma lost a dollar
today. You should
ask if it is hers.

Needs and Wants

Lesson 2

Vocabulary

needs

shelter

wants

flow chart

Reading Skill

Sequence

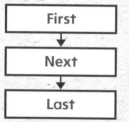

First

↓

Next

↓

Last

Things We Need

Things we must have to live are called **needs**. People have many needs. They need food to eat, water to drink, and clothes to wear. Love and care are needs, too.

People also need **shelter**. A shelter is a place where someone lives. Your home is a shelter.

 What are things people need?

Things We Want

Things we don't need, but would like to have, are called **wants**. We cannot have everything we want. We have to make choices.

Ana and Berta are sisters. They want to buy a doll. Ana has $5. Berta has $4.

A **flow chart** shows the order in which things happen. The flow chart above shows how Ana and Berta made a choice.

 Why did Ana and Berta buy the doll that cost $9?

Check Understanding

1. **Vocabulary** What is a **shelter**?

2. **Sequence** How did Ana and Berta make a choice?

First
↓
Next
↓
Last

3. How are needs and wants different?

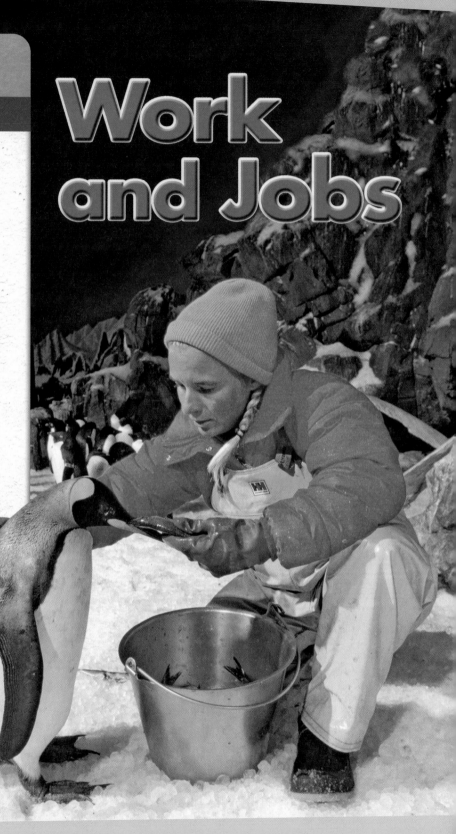

Vocabulary

work

service

volunteer

Reading Skill

Sequence

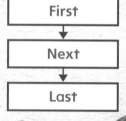

| First |
| Next |
| Last |

Work and Jobs

Why People Work

Work is a job that a person does. People care about their work. They get money for the work they do. People use money to buy the things they need and want.

There are many kinds of work. Some people drive trucks. Some care for others. Some work in offices. Some people have jobs working in a zoo!

 Why do most people work?

Service Jobs

A **service** is work done to help others. School workers, such as teachers and crossing guards, are service workers. They are paid for the services they do.

Some service workers make our world a better place to live. Firefighters and police officers risk their lives to keep us safe. They help people in trouble.

 How do workers help in a community?

Event
Putting Out Fires

These firefighters are putting out a dangerous fire. They are helping us stay safe.

Volunteers

Some people work for free. People who work for free are called **volunteers**. They like to help others.

Mrs. Kent is a volunteer. She cares about dogs. Every day she walks dogs for an animal shelter.

Some volunteers work to help children to read and write. Marla helps Mia read every Tuesday afternoon.

 What do volunteers do?

Check Understanding

1. **Vocabulary** What is **work**?

2. **Sequence** Plan a volunteer class clean up. What should happen first? Next? Last?

First
↓
Next
↓
Last

3. Why is service work important?

Map and Globe Skills

Use a Map Key

Vocabulary

symbol

map key

A **symbol** is something that stands for something else. The 🍎 is a symbol for an apple.

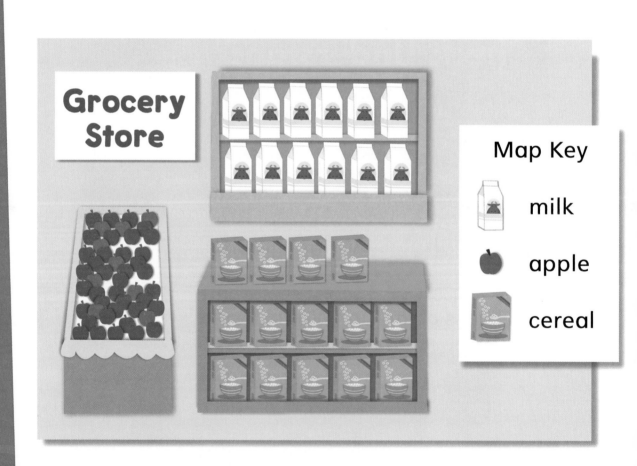

Grocery Store

Map Key

milk

apple

cereal

The small box on the map is called a **map key**. A map key tells you what the symbols on the map mean.

Look at the map of the grocery store on page 20. Find the symbol and the word for apple in the map key. Next, find the apples on the map.

on page 20

Try the Skill

1. What does the **symbol** mean?

2. How many boxes of cereal are on the map?

 Writing Activity Draw a map of a store near you. Make a map key for your map.

All About Goods

Vocabulary

goods

factory

trade

Reading Skill

Sequence

First
Next
Last

Making Goods

Goods are things people grow or make to sell. Farmers grow goods like beans, corn, and strawberries to sell.

Some goods are made in a building called a **factory**. Factory workers run machines to make the goods.

This factory worker is checking the tennis balls. He wants to make sure they are ready for people to buy!

 What are goods?

Trading Goods

Trade means to give something and get something in return. These children are trading toy cars.

Countries trade, too. But, when countries trade, they buy and sell goods. The United States buys airplanes from France. France buys computers from us.

 What does the United States trade with France?

Around the World

The United States trades with Argentina. Argentina sells grapes to us. We sell televisions to Argentina.

Making Work Easier

Long ago, people had to work very hard to grow goods. They dug up the ground and planted seeds by hand.

People
Johnny Appleseed

Johnny Appleseed planted apple trees by hand in the states of Indiana, Illinois, and Ohio. He said, "Nothing gives more yet asks for less than . . . an apple tree."

Today, people use tractors to dig the ground. They use machines to plant the seeds. Machines make our work better and easier.

 How do new machines help us?

Check Understanding

1. **Vocabulary** What is a **factory**?

2. **Sequence** How did planting seeds change from long ago to today?

First
Next
Last

3. Why do we trade?

Vocabulary

Number a paper from I to 3. Next to each number write the word that matches the meaning.

trade   **wants**   **service**

1. things we don't need, but would like to have

2. give something and get something in return

3. work done to help others

Critical Thinking

4. How do we get what we need or want?

5. What would you like to do as a volunteer?

Map and Globe Skills

Look at the map of the grocery store. The map key shows what they sell.

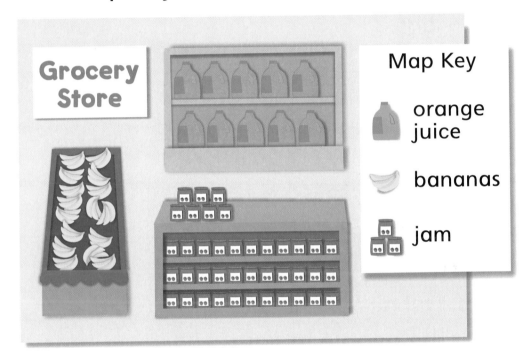

6. What can you buy at the store?

A. rugs, bananas, and jam

B. beans, orange juice, and jam

C. jam, orange juice, and bananas

Economics Activity

Make a Book About Work

1 Draw pictures of people working at different jobs.

2 Write the names of the jobs under the pictures.

3 Make a cover for your book.

4 Tell about the work the people in your book do.

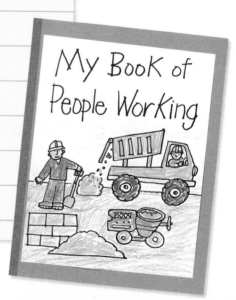

My Book of People Working

Workers Everywhere!

Characters

chef

doctor

police officer

baseball player

lawyer

dancer

Narrator

Workers help and workers care.
Workers are found everywhere!
Name the workers that you see.
Which one would you like to be?

Police Officer

I keep the city safe for you.
I make sure laws are followed, too.
Don't talk to strangers that you see.
If you are lost, please come to me!
I answer calls from 911.
I will not stop until I'm done!

Chef

I will make the meals for you.
Do you like soup or barbecue?
I cut up veggies, chop, and dice.
I want to make your food look nice.
I fry and stir and bake and roast.
I'll spread some jelly on your toast!

Baseball player

I practice hitting balls to you.
I run the bases. Yes, I do!
I learn some rules that I must know.
I exercise from head to toe!
It's time to play, so let's begin.
It's teamwork that will help us win!

Lawyer

I go to court and work each day.
I meet the judge without delay.
I help protect your every right.
I research laws both day and night.
I find what's wrong and speak out, too!
I make things fair. That's what I do!

Dancer

I spin and twirl and do a split.
I jump and whirl and never sit!
I put on costumes for the shows.
I dance around on my tiptoes.
I practice every dance I do.
The music keeps me right on cue!

Doctor

You come to me if you're not well,
with chicken pox or if you fell!
I might tell you to take a rest,
when you are feeling not your best.
It is my job to care for you,
and get you well. That's what I do!

Readers Theater Activity

There are many jobs for you.
Just think what you would
like to do.
Choose a job and act it out.
Tell us what it's all about.
Draw a picture, show it now.
When you're done, please
take a bow!

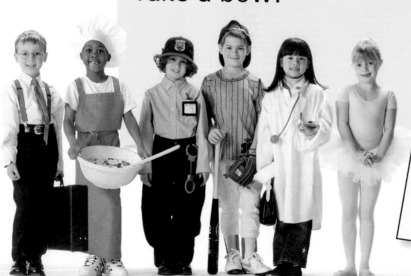

I want to be
a firefighter.

Picture Glossary

F

factory A **factory** is a building where goods are made. (page 23)

flow chart A **flow chart** is a chart that shows the order in which things happen. (page 12)

G

goods **Goods** are things that are made or grown for people to buy. (page 23)

M

map key A **map key** tells what the symbols on a map mean. (page 21)

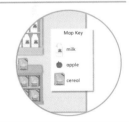

M

money **Money** is something you use to buy things. Money can be paper bills or coins. (page 5)

N

needs **Needs** are things we must have to live. (page 11)

S

save To **save** means to put something away to use later. (page 6)

service A **service** is work done to help others. (page 16)

shelter A **shelter** is a place where someone lives. (page 11)

symbol A **symbol** is something that stands for something else. (page 20)

T

trade To **trade** is to give something and get something in return. (page 24)

V

volunteer A **volunteer** is a person who works for free to help others. (page 18)

W

wants **Wants** are things we do not need but would like to have. (page 12)

work **Work** is a job that someone does. (page 15)

Index

This index lists many things you can find in your book. It tells the page numbers on which they are found. If you see the letter *m* before a page number, you will find a map on that page.

Credits